Loneliness:
The Pathway to Discovery

By Linda McBurney-Gunhouse

Published by:
Creative Focus Publishing
Winnipeg Beach, Manitoba
Canada

Cover Artwork by Linda McBurney- Gunhouse
ISBN: 978-1-928071-25-9
Copyright © 2006 Linda McBurney- Gunhouse
Reprinted 2025
All Rights Reserved.
R1.3

Published by:
Creative Focus Publishing
Box 704
Winnipeg Beach, Manitoba R0C 3G0 Canada
info@creativefocus.ca

Please visit our website:
www.creativefocus.ca

All Scripture is taken from the King James Version of the Bible
unless otherwise stated.

A Note from the Author

Loneliness: The Pathway to Discovery is a result of spending many hours and even years (all counted up) struggling with loneliness. But what was once a painful and difficult experience to endure is now, at times, a welcome friend. How did I get to this place? That's what this book is all about. Within it's pages, you'll discover, as I did, that the state of loneliness is not something that cannot be endured, but rather it is often a doorway to the next step on our journey though life. Unlike other books about loneliness you may have read, this one has as its foundation some pretty powerful Biblical principles that work. It also offers some wonderful practical ideas for dealing with loneliness that have proven successful.

As you read through the pages, I pray that your spiritual eyes will open to your own situation, whatever that may be, and that you will discover the great hope that awaits you. I also pray that you will share what you learn and that in the sharing, you will find more encouragement, strength for your journey, and new friendships that will arise out of your caring. I leave you with a favourite passage of Scripture:

Psalm 126

When the LORD turned again the captivity of Zion, we were like them that dream. Then was our mouth filled with laughter, and our tongue with singing: then said they among the heathen, The LORD hath done great things for them. The LORD hath done great things for us; whereof we are glad. Turn again our captivity, O LORD, as the streams in the south. They that sow in tears shall reap in joy. He that goeth forth and weepeth, bearing precious seed, shall doubtless come again with rejoicing, bringing his sheaves with him.

Linda McBurney-Gunhouse
Winnipeg Beach, MB
Canada

Contents

I would like to thank all the people in my life who have been an incredible support to me and been there for me more times than I can ever count — my husband Craig, my family, and numerous friends and relatives. God Bless each and every one of you.

Most of all, I'd like to give credit where credit is due for all the words and ideas in this book — my Lord and Savior Jesus Christ. May He be praised forever and ever for taking me on an incredible journey of discovery through my many times of loneliness and for turning my sorrow into joy. Amen

Introduction

It is commonly known among writers and would-be writers that you should always write about what you know about. If you know a lot about a particular subject, then you will be qualified to write about it, and you can pass on your expert knowledge so that readers can learn something from your expertise. I would never have volunteered to become an expert at understanding loneliness, but this is something I have experienced for most of my life. So I would like to share what I know and some insights and experiences I have learned so far, in the great hopes that someone reading this will find a new hope and practical answers for this often debilitating human state we find ourselves in.

Loneliness might be something we often don't even stop to think about because we are busy for the most part. But there are times we are acutely aware of the emptiness we feel, and we'd do anything to not have to go through this unpleasant experience. Yet, if we find ourselves feeling lonely more often than not, then many times there is a pattern or reason for it, and this is something we need to look at. This book attempts to do just that — discover how loneliness can lead to a whole new understanding of ourselves and God, and it also offers effective ways to communicate with people. Hence, the title depicts the contents of the book as a "pathway to discovery" rather than trying to explain ways to try to escape loneliness altogether. We may even surprisingly find that, rather than shun loneliness, it will be something we learn to embrace once we see the many positive aspects and opportunities it can and does present to us.

Whether you feel the pain of loneliness or not, I pray that this book will be a great blessing to you as you seek to discover all that life has in store for you. I also hope you will find peace and acceptance as you discover more about solutions that really do work once you try them and apply them. I leave you with a wonderful passage of Scripture that has been a great comfort to me:

> *Whither shall I go from thy spirit? or whither shall I flee from thy presence? If I ascend up into heaven, thou art there: if I make my bed in hell, behold, thou art there. If I take the wings of the morning, and dwell in the uttermost parts of the sea; Even there shall thy hand lead me, and thy right hand shall hold me. If I say, Surely the darkness shall cover me; even the night shall be light about me. Yea, the darkness hideth not from thee; but the night shineth as the day: the darkness and the light are both alike to thee. For thou hast possessed my reins: thou hast covered me in my mother's womb. I will praise thee; for I am fearfully and wonderfully made: marvellous are thy works; and that my soul knoweth right well. Psalm 139:7-14*

Chapter 1
Face to Face with Loneliness

Personal Journey

My first real bout with loneliness came after my sister, two years older than I, graduated from Grade 12 and moved away from home. We had grown up together and shared everything, even a bedroom, until my brother moved away when I was about nine or ten years old. Marlene is the kind of popular, cheery-hearted person anyone would love to have as a sister. Outgoing, smart, and generous to a fault, I always looked up to her and wanted to go everywhere she went. We were playmates until we reached our teen years; then we started to slowly go our separate ways. Psychologists have a term they call "separation anxiety," a condition we find ourselves in when someone close to us is taken away, either from death, a move, or a broken relationship. I certainly felt that, although I didn't know there was a name for it.

The disarming thing about loneliness is that it kind of creeps up on you. You might anticipate it, but you can't fully understand it until you meet it face-to-face; then it seems like a giant that won't go away — larger than life, menacing, and a pest. After my sister moved away, I remember that my parents made special efforts to include me more in their life. We took trips together, shopped together, talked more together, walked together, cooked meals together, and generally, since I was their youngest daughter still at home, our family became re-invented from six to only three. There were a lot of adjustments to make. Along with my sister moving away, many of her friends who were also my close friends, moved away, got married, and started to lead lives of their own outside of the school social circle. So being shy and unsure of what to do without my big sister to guide me along, I

3

had to learn to make new friends with kids my own age and younger. Being a very stressful time, this is when I started becoming dependent on drugs and sometimes alcohol. Then when I moved away from home two years later, these dependencies escalated, as I've shared in another book I wrote called *When Love Is All There Is*.

But there are many different situations that bring people face to face with loneliness. It could be when someone dies, or friends move away or get married. It could be even because of being considered the wrong color (Black or White), race, religion, or from coming from the wrong scale on the social ladder. In my hometown, for example, there was a social scale. Even though it may not have been obvious, still there was an awareness of it. Social classes exist everywhere: cities and towns and even villages — from the very wealthy to the middle class to the lower income. There is also a definite hierarchy in every kind of employment imaginable. We see it in offices, businesses, and hospitals where doctors come first, then the various levels of nurses, technicians, and so on. Friendship circles can exclude you if you don't fit exactly into their idea of social aptness. Everyone seems to be slotted somewhere, and this can not only create an incredible feeling of inadequacy (depending on the situation), but also one of loneliness if a person feels ostracized because they are left out of certain social situations. If a person is shy, this only exacerbates the feeling of not fitting in since many people (who are outgoing) may not bother to try and draw out a shy person and try to make friends with him or her.

I can't say that the loneliness I felt at 15 was the same as the loneliness I felt once I left home and was on my own. Nor was it the same as I felt as a married woman. It seems to come in different stages of my life, and I am always challenged by it, but rather than a huge giant that can't be felled, I realize that it will be a time of personal growth, and with every spurt of growth, there are growing pains that will hopefully lead to a better me.

I have to admit that loneliness isn't always something that just suddenly happens and creeps up on me unawares. It is something I've often chosen, because of the type of work I enjoy and because of the type of person I am. I enjoy the quiet beauty of solitude when my mind is calm and I am unafraid, when I am in an almost euphoric state of mind, and then I start creating — perhaps a story, poem, painting, sewing, or jewelry creation. But this can't really be defined as loneliness, although I am alone. There is nothing painful or distressful about it. Loneliness is when we feel acute pain and longing to be with other people, and for some reason or another, we are unable to achieve that meaningful interaction we want and need with another human being.

When I was single, I couldn't imagine that married people ever felt lonely. After all, they had each other all the time. But I found out that without meaningful communication and shared goals, and working at spending valuable time together, that a loneliness worse than singlehood would be inevitable. Worse because the expectation of having a fulfilling relationship with your spouse is never quite reached, at least without a lot of concerted effort and shared planning. In my case, we moved from the city to a small resort town one hour north of the city. Being a writer, the quiet setting and beautiful scenery was perfect for writing and other creative pursuits like painting and photography. But every morning when I'd wake up and my husband would already be gone to work, I immediately felt a loss and a loneliness that I wouldn't see him until much later in the day. I still go through bouts of loneliness, but it does not bother me nearly as much as it used to.

What is Loneliness?

Everyone will experience loneliness at one time or another in their lifetime, whether married or single. And living in a rural setting where there are fewer people and less opportunity to socialize with doesn't explain why statistics have shown that there are more lonely people in the cities than anywhere else. We don't have to look far to discover that loneliness plagues our present-day society, and perhaps even more so in this highly technological world, where workers choose to work from home, with the only connection to people via the internet and telephone wires. Statistics also show that even though millions of people suffer with loneliness, it is still difficult to find feasible ways of dealing with it. In fact, in researching the topic over many years, I found very few books that went beyond the surface of defining it and offering practical help for it. The reason some of the more obvious suggestions were not long-lasting is that psychology deals with it from the perspective of the soul rather than the spirit. While it is easy enough to define loneliness — *without companionship, solitary, feeling of isolation, being lonely and alone* — it is much more difficult to find the root causes without delving into it further.

I believe it is basically a spiritual problem that is manifest through the soul, and this is what fools people and makes finding the root cause and cure somewhat elusive. People often think it is an emotion; they "feel lonely," so try to fix it through temporary means, mainly through avenues of the soul: with our mind and will, or willpower. The fixes are temporary since we mistakenly believe that other people are the ultimate cure. People then start to become real estate — we want them and covet them, wanting people so much in our lives that they become a commodity. So we become self-centered and our goal is, "I need people for what they can do for me," rather than "What can I do for other people?" Some people call this co-dependency, another important topic that many books have been written about.

I find it exciting that if we look at loneliness from a spiritual perspective, rather than as a natural condition of man, we can begin to find some real answers that often surround its complexities. From the very beginning of creation, when sin entered people's hearts, there was an immediate separation from God. This led to fear, insecurity, and the greatest devastation of all, loneliness. If we believe that we were created for companionship and relationship with God Himself, then until we meet with Him on a meaningful level, no person in the world will suffice: loneliness will be inevitable. We'll cover more of this in the next chapter.

Different Kinds of Loneliness

Not all loneliness is negative. Some people make some of the biggest contributions to humankind when they are alone and concentrating on the task at hand. We need to see the distinction between being alone and loneliness, and there is a substantial difference.

Loneliness by Default

Sometimes we find ourselves alone by default, which means that something happens beyond our control, and we come face-to-face with loneliness. This is what happened to me when my sister left home and moved away. Sometimes a loved one may pass away suddenly, and we find ourselves alone. There will be times, even though we have friends, everyone is busy at the same time, and no one is available to even talk to. Also, a move to a new place can cause loneliness until we start getting involved in church, sports, or other social outlets. Many people with illnesses and also elderly people suffer with loneliness when they are unable to get out to socialize. People in nursing homes and hospitals sometimes do not get any visitors other than the staff working there. Young people may feel ostracized by peers because they are different or are new to their school or area, and so they will also feel loneliness. One of the most painful types of loneliness is the feeling that we just don't fit in anywhere, as hard as we may try. Everyone will experience some type of loneliness at some point in their lives since so many inevitable events may happen.

Loneliness by Profession

Could you ever believe that loneliness can be a passageway to many open doors and that sometimes there is no other way offered that will lead to the open door you have been praying for and hoping for? Writing books is a lonely business, I can tell you. I am just now finally writing the many books I've had in mind to write for almost 30 years. I know why it's taken me this long — every time I sat down to write, I'd write for only so long, then look out the window at the sun shining, and I'd hear the birds singing, and I'd want to be outside or go for a walk or do anything to get away from the strict discipline of researching and writing. My house has been cleaned many times over because I couldn't sit behind the computer long enough to finish a story. I don't like to be alone, yet my life's calling requires me to be alone so that I can share my thoughts with people that will one day appreciate my books and be helped by them (at least I hope and pray).

Mothers or fathers of small children might be in a similar situation. They are alone all day raising their children, and this is an even greater commitment since they are shaping, molding, and teaching the next generation and preparing them to go out into the world one day where, hopefully, their lives will positively impact others.

People who do great things make the sacrifice of being alone in order to accomplish what needs to be done. Think of the greatest inventors, scientists, and doctors, who sacrificed hours and years of their time to give us what we have today — computers, airplanes, electricity, penicillin, and countless other necessary things we now take for granted. Every profession demands hours and years of study to become a professional. I spent eight years alone studying to obtain my Bachelor of Arts and Bachelor of Education degree. And I just scratched the surface. Loneliness, because of a profession or long-term goal, can be a very good and healthy thing because, although it may take some time, the end results will be good. A doctor, for example, will sacrifice at least seven difficult years learning the profession, and then he or she will likely spend a lifetime helping to cure people and even save some lives. We wouldn't want him or her studying for any less since we are trusting them with our very lives. And pharmacy is the same — we want to know the pharmacist is dispensing the right drugs for our particular illness or ailment.

Loneliness by Choice

There is another type of loneliness that is unhealthy. Sometimes we choose to become reclusive and want to avoid people because we may have been hurt and feel angry, abandoned, abused, and so on. But in this situation, the only person that really suffers is ourselves. Choosing to cut ourselves loose from people for whatever reason can be potentially harmful since statistics show that social isolation can lead to heart problems, high blood pressure, mental problems, drug and alcohol dependency, gambling and other addictions, and in some cases, even suicide.

Then there are people that look like they have all the friends in the world, but when they get home and no one is there, are faced with a worse loneliness than someone who is deemed to be rejected by society or someone overcome by debilitating addictions. These people are often the life of the party, but secretly they are afraid to develop honest, open, and intimate relationships with other people.

Some people may choose loneliness because they just don't want to take time to pursue and maintain friendships. Rather than turn to harmful addictions, they may become a workaholic, a term we often applaud in our work-oriented society. While it is a wonderful thing to enjoy our profession or job, when it begins to take over our lives, it is most often our family that pays the price. Some children are raised by only one parent because the other parent is either away on business, working late at the office, or unavailable for quality time when he/she gets home because they're too tired to deal with family matters. Sometimes marriages end when one or both partners are too involved in their careers. It is easy to lose track of friends as we launch into the various phases of life and try to balance hectic careers with marriage and family relationships, plus keep other special interest commitments going.

For whatever reason a person chooses loneliness, there is no substitution for our need for people and God by using things or even too much activity as a way to try and deal with it.

In the next chapter, we'll look at what really lies at the heart of loneliness, and we'll find some remarkable truths that will begin to help us make some sense of loneliness.

Chapter 2
At the Heart of Loneliness

At the heart of my loneliness was a feeling of inadequacy — that I didn't count and wasn't as important as others. So I found myself not only dealing with loneliness but also with low self-esteem. Low self-esteem can and does have a crippling effect on our social life and all our relationships. I must confess that all the while growing up, I felt that my sister Marlene was a much more popular person than I — she did well in school, had her pick of friends and boyfriends, was generous and hospitable, and she knew how to communicate with people and put them at ease. I, on the other hand, was painfully shy, introverted, and sensitive, and I didn't deal as well with all the social complexities involved in friendships and socializing with people. When we had company over and if there were other kids, I was always relieved when they left and there was just my sister and me again. I loved to play every kind of childhood game, swim in the summer, and then in the winter toboggan, skate and snowmobile, but my mind was almost always focused towards the creative. This made me feel that I was different than the other kids — more quiet and reflective. Even as a child, I loved reading and writing and couldn't wait to begin writing in my own diary. I excelled in all my language arts courses and later in English. In my teen years, I spent time alone daily, writing in my diary, while everyone else was downstairs still at the dinner table, chatting, laughing, and then doing the dishes.

After moving away from home at the age of 17 and feeling an acute sense of displacement and anxiety, a new feeling of loneliness washed over me. But at that time I had none of the tools to deal with it as I have today. That first year away from home for the first time, and by a series of bad choices I had made, led to me having a nervous breakdown that same year. Although I was a Christian since the age of five, I had strayed far away from the God of my childhood. Many years later, while writing a paper on terrorism for a university course in Political Studies, I was shocked to discover that most terrorists join a group because they are lonely and looking for a place to fit in. Also, the need to belong is so powerful that some people will stop at nothing in order to feel accepted, that they matter, and that they are needed. People that join cults have exactly the same needs — they may have been rejected by others and abandoned by society or even the church in some cases, and so will gladly accept the hand of friendship from the first convincing voice that comes along. I have to say, I fit that category during that first year away from home. And since I had strayed so far away from God, the lines between right and wrong, truth and a lie were so blurred that I justified every compromise of my faith.

The Roots of Loneliness

In my 20s, when I was trying to establish a career, find a place in the city to settle, and develop longer-term friendships, I found myself feeling not only lost and confused, but I was lonely again. I had already had a huge change of heart and life from my experiences in a Saskatchewan based Bible school following that first year away from home, but loneliness was still a reality that I felt inept to deal with. When I was on my days off or between office jobs, I'd go to one of my favourite places, the local library, and spend time searching the self-help and psychology sections looking for books on depression, anxiety, and loneliness. At that time, there were no books on loneliness that really interested me. Besides, if they weren't written from a Biblical or Christian perspective, I felt that they would be lacking. While some of the self-help books did give me further understanding into my situation, I found a much better source to help me — the Bible.

Searching the Scriptures really opened my eyes to the truth about loneliness and the truth about myself. I made some discoveries that changed my thinking and changed the course of my life. For one thing, I discovered that Jesus completely identified with me in my feelings of loneliness, and that He Himself had felt that way and feels at times like we do. Scripture makes this abundantly clear.[1]

I discovered that the God of all creation came to this earth to die for our sins and rise again triumphant so that He could defeat death and all the powers of Satan. He also came to bridge the gap between us and Him so that we could enjoy a close relationship with Him. He did this by experiencing all the same things that we do so that He could completely understand and relate to what we go through in these human sinful bodies (yet He was without sin). He is not a stranger to suffering and sorrow, as Isaiah 58 indicates. The only difference is that His suffering and sorrow wasn't for Himself, but for you and me. He felt the full weight of not only our sin, but the effects of it as well — our sorrows, troubles, sicknesses, and all the psychological distresses we feel, like guilt, anger, regret, unforgiveness, and so on. He also feels our loneliness, feelings of inadequacy and rejection, and He knows our deepest needs whatever they may be. Hebrews 4:15 and 16 describes it well:

> *For we have not an high priest which cannot be touched with the feeling of our infirmities; but was in all points tempted like as we are, yet without sin. Let us therefore come boldly unto the throne of grace, that we may obtain mercy, and find grace to help in time of need. Hebrews 4:15-16*

Another favourite verse that greatly helped me, also found in Hebrews:

> *I will never leave thee, nor forsake thee. (Hebrews 13:5b)*

If we think about it, there is nothing that the Lord can't handle. He understands us, and He knows what we need. People don't know

---

[1] Read Isaiah 58:2-8, Hebrew 4:15, John 16:32a (all the disciples scatter and leave Him alone).

what we need, and even if we want them to, they can't possibly meet all our needs; only God can and wants to, and will.

This was the first revelation that began to change my life — that Jesus completely understood me like no one else ever could, and that He cared enough about me to SHARE in my sorrow and loneliness. I would be comforted to know from that point on that I AM NEVER TRULY ALONE for the rest of my life! Some people may struggle with trusting in a God they can neither see nor understand and wonder how He can dispel the loneliness we feel, but that doesn't mean the Lord won't make Himself known to us. The children of Israel struggled with the very same thing even though God visibly led them through the wilderness by cloud and fire. It all has to do with faith.

The second thing I learned, and this was the life-changing part, is that my loneliness had little to do with me. It might have to do with temporary circumstances, but it had nothing to do with me as a person. In other words, the feeling of inadequacy, insecurity, and that I am not good enough or as good as others was really a lie from Satan. This insidious lie is clever because, rather than believing it is a lie, we take ownership of it, and this keeps us from believing the truth about ourselves according to God's perspective. We start to live up to what we believe about ourselves. This Scripture supports the fact that Satan accuses us:

> *And I heard a loud voice saying in heaven, Now is come salvation, and strength, and the kingdom of our God, and the power of his Christ: for the accuser of our brethren is cast down, which accused them before our God day and night. Revelation 12:10*

I discovered that because I identify with Christ and am His child, I am a target for every kind of attack possible from Satan because Satan hates God and all His children and also hates the truth. He loves nothing more than to kick us down and make us feel inadequate, insecure, timid, and introspective to keep us from spreading this amazing Gospel or Good News of God's love and salvation to all who'll believe and receive it. This is also recorded in Scripture. A wonderful verse I've quoted and confessed many times when under such an attack is:

> *Ye are of God, little children, and have overcome them: because <u>greater is he that is in you, than he that is in the world</u>. 1 John 4:4*

And this knowledge led to a third, most powerful and profound realization: since the Holy Spirit indwells me, this means that He is fully equipped to deal with every single situation in my life, whether it's loneliness, illness, grief, confusion, depression, or any number of problems that may arise. All I need to do is go to Him in prayer and hand it over to Him. Some people make the mistake of asking God to help them overcome loneliness or some other ailment. But the truth is, when Jesus died on the cross, He had already overcome it years before it was felt or experienced by that person. Until I believed this with all my heart, soul, and mind, I failed at every attempt to overcome loneliness and all the other seemingly insurmountable problems in my life. Remember in Chapter One, I said that if we look at loneliness from a spiritual perspective, rather than a natural condition of man, we can begin to find some real answers that often surround its complexities. Can you start to see how the only effective way you can deal with loneliness is to hand it over completely to God and let Him carry the full weight of it?

But this doesn't mean that we will never feel lonely again. It does mean that we don't have to be swallowed up by it. When we believe the Lord is with us, loves us, cares enough about us to feel our pain, and that HE HAS THE ABILITY AND IS WILLING to take the full weight of the loneliness we feel, then we will never again suffer from the ill-effects of loneliness in the same way because we know we are never truly alone. Jesus was alone many times in His earthly ministry, but if we look carefully at Scripture, He said that He was never alone because His Father was with Him.[2] There are times we may forget that the Lord is with us and neglect to read His many promises, but this is our own error. The Lord will meet us when we make a concerted effort to meet Him through prayer.

Why does God allow Loneliness?

There is a great cost to being a follower of the Lord Jesus, and loneliness is often a natural result of following Him. In fact, if we have come from an ungodly lifestyle, it doesn't take us long after we become Christians to start to feel lonely, especially if any of our unsaved friends and relatives begin to shun us or make fun of us. This is when some Christians fall — feeling the rejection because now they are "different" or a "holy roller," they can't handle being ostracized and excluded from the old gang, so they go back to their former life. While they remain saved, they start to backslide and perhaps keep their faith quiet so they won't upset anyone's apple cart, so to speak. Yet, Scripture is clear — there is a cost to serving the Lord, and we need to make an all-out commitment to Him, in spite of rejection, if we truly call ourselves Christians:

> *As they were walking along the road, a man said to him, "I will follow you wherever you go." Jesus replied, "Foxes have holes and birds of the air have nests, but the Son of Man has no place to lay his head." He said to another man, "Follow me." But the man replied, "Lord, first let me go and bury my father." Jesus said to him, "Let the dead bury their own dead, but you go and proclaim the kingdom of God." Still another said, "I will follow you, Lord; but first let me go back and say good bye to my family." Jesus replied, "No one who puts his hand to the plow and looks back is fit for service in the kingdom of God." Luke 9:57-62*

---

[2] See John 8:16, 29, 16:32.

16

Whoever does forsake their former life for the sake of the Lord and His Kingdom is promised great reward.[3] There are many other verses that encourage us to take a stand even if it means rejection and persecution. One of the more important ones is for the sake of the lost:

> *But if our gospel be hid, it is hid to them that are lost: In whom the god of this world hath blinded the minds of them which believe not, lest the light of the glorious gospel of Christ, who is the image of God, should shine unto them. 2 Corinthians 4:3-4*

Our temporary discomfort is just that — temporary. But for those who don't know Christ, their discomfort is eternal.

Also, God allows us to go through loneliness since sometimes it's the only way He can get our attention. This is how He first got my attention. While a student at Bible school, I struggled with many issues, mainly with making an all-out commitment to the Lord Jesus and to allow Him to become Lord of my life, rather than continuing on my own way with me in the driver's seat. I had to have everything, all the props, taken away in order to give my full attention to the Lord and get to know Him for who He is. I would go for long walks down a deserted highway on the bare prairies of north-western Saskatchewan. There wasn't a tree in sight, and I got a full view of the vast round horizon. Sometimes I'd enjoy a spectacular pastel sunrise and other times a blazing, fiery orange and navy crested sunset. At night the stars would glitter from the heights of the heavens to the base of the horizon all around, and it was so bright you wouldn't need a flashlight since no trees or clouds obscured the full moon.

During these times the Lord would teach me things, and we'd plan for my future, as He'd give me glimpses into what He had in store for me after Bible school. One night He filled me with the

---

[3] See Matthew 19:29

outpouring of the Holy Spirit and I began to speak with other tongues. Following this was a time of great growth and more healing. My ministry of exhortation began, and my writing changed — instead of bringing attention to myself, it was now directed to glorify Him and also to help others. I lost myself in His glorious presence and found a new freedom in my faith.

Many times since then, being alone has been a blessed time because I am always assured that it's temporary, and it's a time to grow and learn deeper lessons. It's taught me patience and to wait on the Lord. Without these many times alone with Him, I wouldn't be where I am today. Sometimes waiting yields the greatest fruit if we just learn to trust in the Father's perfect timing, and we do not rush out on our own unprepared for all that life may throw at us.

In the next chapter, we'll look at relationships and how they can make or break us. We'll discover what makes relationships work and how to have meaningful fellowship with others.

Chapter 3
Healthy Relationships

It took me many years to discover what a healthy relationship looks like, and also what can happen when we pursue something outside of God's perfect will and timing. When it comes to loneliness, I learned that patience was one of God's top priorities for me to learn. Patience and waiting on the Lord is a priceless thing — I only wish I would have learned it much earlier on in my life, for I know I would have been spared much heartache and sorrow.

When I was 26, I felt that I was ready to get married and so, in haste, almost made one of the biggest mistakes of my whole life. I had met Eric[4] at a Bible study at the Pentecostal church I was attending at the time. The pastor of the church called me a few days later and asked if it was alright with me if Eric gave me a call to meet me for coffee. At the time, I had been living alone for two years and really struggling with loneliness since my sister, who had also been my roommate for four and a half years, had gotten married two years earlier. Some of my other close friends had gotten married or were also getting married. Feeling vulnerable and that I was missing the boat, I was anxious to meet someone, especially a nice Christian man. So I agreed to meet Eric for coffee.

I found out that Eric was from Ontario and had just moved to Winnipeg. He was looking for help and support, so he called the 100 Huntley 1-800 line and hooked up with this Pentecostal church. He shared that he had come out of a life of drug dependency and alcoholism and was now recovered and wanting to start life over. I wasn't particularly attracted to Eric at first because he seemed

---

[4] Not his real name

nervous, and this made it really difficult to communicate with him. I should have seen the signs right then and ended it before it went any further. But desperate people do desperate things. He called me again and seemed more relaxed, and thinking he was now being himself, I decided to meet him once more. Not wanting to face loneliness, I spent many more times with him after that over the course of about a month — we went to the movies, to the park, out for dinner, for coffee, to church, and so on. He seemed sincere, would write me romantic cards, and buy me beautiful gifts even though he wasn't working at the time. He seemed to know the right thing to say and the right gift to give just when I needed it. I was really enjoying my time with Eric, and my feelings grew from like to love — I thought that maybe he was the one. We seemed made for each other; at least this is what he kept telling me. Wanting to believe he was the right one so I wouldn't have to face the loneliness of being single, a short time later, I agreed to marry him.

About a month after we'd been seeing each other, Eric called me one night, and he sounded different — he'd been drinking. My heart sank. I was so shocked and angry, I told him never to call me when he was drunk. I hung up the phone and felt my heart break, so I cried and cried. Had I been duped into thinking he had changed when all along, he hadn't? I knew in my heart I couldn't be involved with this man, yet the relationship, or what was left of it, went on for another five months or so.

I can tell you that they were the rockiest, most painful five months of my entire life. Rather than break up as my heart was telling me to do, I got the idea that I could change him. I somehow still believed that he was the right one, even though my heart was broken and would break again and again during those months. I found out that not only was he drinking, but he was doing drugs, having wild parties, seeing other women for one night stands, and worse. All this time, the tender love I had for him was, I believe, a sincere, godly love, and he was taking full advantage of my weakness for him and the need to love someone.

Finally, a concerned family member told me straight to have nothing more to do with Eric, that he was trouble, would be abusive, and that if I married him, I would live to regret it. Still, I couldn't believe that Eric was that kind of man. Sure, he had his bad habits, but when he was sober and drug-free, he was the most loving, compassionate person I had ever known. This was the side of him I had fallen in love with, and I wasn't ready to give him up, but I kept hoping and believing his bad side would disappear. But of course it didn't. I lived a roller coaster ride for the next few months, hoping he'd change and despairing when he didn't.

The relationship was so topsy-turvy and emotionally consuming that during this time I was unable to work, and my sister was kind enough to let me live in her spacious basement that had a private washroom and two bedrooms. I found comfort in her love and kindness while going through a bottoming out in my life. One day, I had an appointment with a social worker to try and collect money for rent and food. The lady asked why I wasn't working, and I told her about Eric. She sat back in her chair and told me he was good-for-nothing and that he didn't love me at all. She said that my life with him would be hell and that he would never be able to love or support me. She told me in no uncertain terms to get rid of him as fast as I can and have nothing more to do with him. She said she'd seen this kind of smooth-talking street person destroy many women's lives, and the best thing is to end it now. It felt like I had been hit with a ton of bricks. At first I wanted to defend myself and Eric, but there was no stopping her. After I left, I thought about what she had said, and I wondered, *How could she have known the kind of man Eric is without ever meeting him?* After the shock wore off, I knew it was a strong warning and a wake-up call. It was what I needed to hear, and she was the second person to warn me about him, so I decided to end it with Eric.

After breaking up with Eric, I started to really realize what I had been saved from, especially when he threatened to take his own life when I refused to get back together with him. He was showing his true colors. Then I was filled with questions: *How could I stoop to this level and throw my pearls before swine?* What had brought me to this point in my life where I was willing to compromise and settle for far less than God's best for me? But in my loneliness and impatience to be married, I realized that rather than truly loving me, Eric had used my weakness and said all the right things that I wanted to hear even though he could never have lived up to his many promises. About three weeks after I broke up with him, a friend told me that he was engaged to a woman he had briefly met in an alcohol rehab centre. I never heard from him again, but it took me months, even years, to recover from this emotionally charged, near-fatal relationship.

I began a quest to discover what had happened, and why I had chosen to get involved with a man who could have destroyed my life. I discovered from other friends and acquaintances, self-help groups, and 12-step groups I attended that there were many other women who were going through or had gone through similar situations. It had a lot to do with low self-esteem and a fear of letting go, believing that someone will change when they clearly will not or cannot without divine intervention. Many women in crisis situations are terrified to break out on their own for fear of what their crazed partner will do in a fit of rage. Some women have small children to think of. The thought of being alone and trying to support oneself (even worse when children are involved) is terrifying indeed. Some women would rather put up with the outbursts of rage and take the abuse than find themselves alone, broke, not knowing where to go. Whether we like to think about it or not, these are real situations all around us.

To learn how to avoid these kinds of relationships altogether, I went for counseling, and I finally found a counselor who said things that made sense to me. The words she used were "cherish" and "respect." If someone cherishes me and respects me, then he is someone who will love me. You can't fake cherishing or respecting someone, because it will flow out of a sincere heart. This is something I began to look for in relationships, and several years later, God did provide a wonderful husband who does cherish and respect me.[5]

Many wrong, harmful, or mismatched relationships have come out of a person's broken life — when they've felt lonely, impatient, angry (sometimes following a sudden death or unexpected break-up), vulnerable, and insecure. Yet, Scripture warns against having relationships with unbelievers (or those who have left the faith) because they will not be on the same wave length. In some cases, they may even try to pull us back into an unhealthy, ungodly lifestyle that serves little purpose except to lead us into much heartache later on. Loneliness will only intensify once we realize the disparity that exists. In Scripture we are warned not to marry or become overly involved with anyone who is not a Bible-believing and Bible-living Christian. There are a number of passages that mention this:

> *Be ye not unequally yoked together with unbelievers: for what fellowship hath righteousness with unrighteousness? and what communion hath light with darkness? 2 Corinthians 6:14*

> *Can two walk together, except they be agreed? Amos 3:3*

> *And have no fellowship with the unfruitful works of darkness, but rather reprove them. Ephesians 5:11*

Even if our relationships are of the right kind, we need to look at what friendship really is and to go even deeper than that, to talk about fellowship.

---

[5] This amazing and miraculous story is written in my book *Journey to Oneness.*

Friendship

There are many different kinds of friendships. We might have a best friend we see regularly, a distant friend we call, text or email, several casual friends, or a group of friends we hang out with. When we think of a friend, we think of someone we share something in common with, someone we enjoy being with, someone we like a lot, and in some cases love. Friends can certainly fill a temporary void when we feel lonely or need companionship. There are also acquaintances, people we know, but we wouldn't consider we know well enough to call a friend. An acquaintance might be our surrounding neighbours, people we see at work, or professional people we turn to, like our hairdresser, electrician, or plumber. Friendships we nurture and spend time developing can become like family to us. They can be there when family can't; they can give us honest and objective advice when needed. Usually, they will always try to be there because their needs match our own, and they will expect the same from us. Sometimes your male or female friend will be the best candidate for your life partner. My husband and I were (and still are) best friends before we got married.

So how come, in this world where friendships are common, and at least everyone has at least one friend they can turn to, are there so many lonely people? I've already shared my experience with meeting the wrong person, and I'm sure there are many stories out there of people in situations that are unbearable because of the difficult person they married and are now stuck with. What happens, other than marrying the wrong kind of person, in a world where friendships abound, that people still feel lonely?

In thinking about this chapter and the whole idea of friendship, and I've had many different friends and been part of a variety of different social groups over the years, another word came to my mind that is rarely used except amongst church-goers and Bible-believing

Christians. That word is "fellowship." Fellowship is not necessarily the same as friendship, but can fulfil in a much deeper way the significant need for people in our lives.

Fellowship

The first I ever heard about this word was at Bible school. The Greek word for it is "koinonia" (correct spelling is koinwniða). As well as fellowship, it means *association, community, communion, joint participation, and intercourse.* The Bible uses the word "fellowship" frequently, as in the following verses:

> *Praying us with much intreaty that we would receive the gift, and take upon us the fellowship of the ministering to the saints. 2 Corinthians 8:4*
>
> *And to make all men see what is the fellowship of the mystery, which from the beginning of the world hath been hid in God, who created all things by Jesus Christ: Ephesians 3:9*
>
> *That which we have seen and heard declare we unto you, that ye also may have fellowship with us: and truly our fellowship is with the Father, and with his Son Jesus Christ. 1 John 1:3*

When we become Christians, we enter into a whole world-wide family of believers. When I first realized this, it was one of the most comforting thoughts I had ever had. This means that wherever I may be in the world, there will always be a family of believers where I will be welcome to go and have fellowship with. I never have to be alone. Yet, in order to really enjoy all the benefits of fellowship with others, it will depend on the degree that we put ourselves and our heart into it — this will determine whether our need for fellowship is met. The more we give of ourselves, the more our needs will be met. Fellowship means community. What a wonderful word, for it implies a group of people all working together for the common good. This is real fellowship because each member cares equally for the needs of one another.

Also, the idea of the family of believers all networking together as the Body of Christ is one that builds each member up, since, according to Scripture, every member has an important part.[6] Regrettably, churches are not perfect because people are not perfect. Sometimes church members play favorites — they elevate one ministry over another, and someone will always feel left out or that their gift is unimportant. Therefore, favouritism will kill fellowship. But the greatest thing that will block fellowship with other believers is when we harbour sin, like unforgiveness and bitterness in our hearts against someone. This also affects our relationship with God, as it says in the following:

> *If we say that we have fellowship with him, and walk in darkness, we lie, and do not the truth: But if we walk in the light, as he is in the light, we have fellowship one with another, and the blood of Jesus Christ his Son cleanseth us from all sin. 1 John 1:6-7*

If we wonder why our relationships aren't fulfilling or may even be non-existent, it is because there are underlying problems of dissension. Hidden sins that we may have excused and even forgotten about need to be brought to light and dealt with so that true and meaningful fellowship with God and others may be restored.

If roots of loneliness are spiritual, then fellowship for every believer is certainly one of the most important tools we have. If we band together and we're willing to truly and humbly serve one another, we will be more likely to avoid the wrong kind of relationships, which is something I should have done.

In the next chapter, we are going to roll up our sleeves and look at some workable and practical ideas to deal with loneliness.

---

[6] See I Corinthians 12:12-27.

Chapter 4
Finding Freedom

In the last chapter, we talked about fellowship as something deeper than friendship and as a significant way to deal with loneliness. But are friendships and fellowship meant only for social gatherings and fun? And do mere social gatherings or evenings out to the movies constitute and build lasting friendships? Certainly not. At least it hasn't worked that way for me, since friendships on this level have often been shallow and unfulfilling. Rather than seek friendships to just be with people, another way that the Bible talks about is to go the next step — to actually go out of our way and look for ways to help and minister to people. This is a sure way to find freedom from the devastating effects and feelings of loneliness.

But I want to make a distinction between just helping others because it's the right thing to do, and ministering to others from a servant-heart. Helping others may be just a sporadic thing where we do a good deed that costs us little or nothing. Ministering to people involves commitment, where it costs us something. It may cost us time, money, a sharing of talents and other gifts, and it will certainly yield far greater benefits than just doing a good deed once in awhile. Not only does it free us from the bondage of focusing only on ourselves and getting our own needs met, but sometimes the people we minister to will become our best friends.

What is Ministry?

In the Biblical context, ministry means to "serve" one another, and it often flows out of a sincere desire to make a positive difference in someone else's life. In fact, ministry is what keeps a fellowship of believers together, and more importantly, ministry is what draws people to the Lord and gives them a chance to receive all the love He has to offer. Because sincere, caring Christians took the time to love me when I was least lovable, I took a second look at Christianity and was so impressed I wanted to know this same God that they believed in. It takes courage to step out of ourselves and our comfort zone and go the extra mile for someone — but this is at the heart of ministry. And when God's love is in our hearts, we will want to share that love in practical and helpful ways to help those in need and help those less fortunate than ourselves.

One of the most surprising passages of Scripture I ever found in the Bible about the very character of Jesus (God in the flesh) is when a woman (called the mother of Zebedee's children) approaches Jesus and asks Him if her two sons can have the honoured place of sitting on either side of Him in His kingdom.[7] Jesus response is that it is not His decision, but His Father in heaven. Then He exhorts His followers to think outside the box — that God's idea of leadership is opposite to man's:

> *But it shall not be so among you: but whosoever will be great among you, let him be your minister; And whosoever will be chief among you, let him be your servant: Even as the Son of man came not to be ministered unto, but to minister, and to give his life a ransom for many. Matthew 20:26-28*

Jesus didn't just command His followers to be servants to others. He demonstrated it in everything He did, the supreme example when He died on the cross for us. What a wonderful thought to focus on when we are feeling the loneliest — Jesus caring for us enough to humble Himself for us to the extent of giving up His own life. This is difficult to fathom, that a holy and sinless God of the entire universe and all created things would stoop to serve fallen man, and that He would die

---

[7] Read this account in Matthew 20:20-28.

for us to pay for our sins and remove the penalty of death from us forever. I'm so glad I know and serve the God of the Hebrew Bible.

Heartfelt Commitment

Of all the good things we can do with our lives, the most rewarding is when we start to make heartfelt commitments for the sake of others. James talks about ministry in the purest sense of the word — when we go out of our way to truly care for the needs of another. This is when God reveals His compassionate heart to us, and those we minister to can see, touch, and feel His love through us.

> *Pure religion and undefiled before God and the Father is this, To visit the fatherless and widows in their affliction, and to keep himself unspotted from the world.*
> *James 1:27*

What great reward when we step outside of our comfort zones and reach out to help another. Sometimes it takes many times to do this before we are completely free of our focus on self. Then we go beyond just helping someone once in awhile, and we find something we can plug into — to become involved and committed to on a more regular basis. This might mean that we volunteer to visit the sick, or we take a meal over to a family who is grieving. When my father passed away, each day that week and beyond, someone in the town brought a full steaming meal to the door ready for us to eat. Sometimes we had lunch and supper delivered all in one day. Our family never had to even think about cooking. People were very loving and supportive, which lightened our load and made us feel so grateful that people were so thoughtful and kind towards us. Their love and care for us literally carried us through each day as we prepared for the funeral.

I could write a book alone on the times people have come through for me, and I knew they had listened to the still small voice of God and

29

ministered to me exactly what I needed. My oldest sister has called me many times and told me God had placed me on her heart. So she'd call when I was the most discouraged, confused, and lonely and give me a word of encouragement. My mom has also spent countless times praying for me, and I wasn't even aware of it. Her and my dad have been a tremendous support to me all my life, providing whatever need they could and especially giving me unending prayer support.

And other than family, I know that there are angels disguised as people all around us who go about doing good and fulfilling the royal law of love according to Scripture.[8] Sometimes they just do a simple thing, like stop traffic to let us cross the street. Sometimes they let us go ahead when we're in a long line-up at the check-out counter and only have one or two items. For some people, doing good and helping others is a way of life — they do it all the time and enjoy going out of their way for someone, partly because they've discovered the great personal reward in doing so. By helping others, we help ourselves.

In the next part, I'd like to discuss several practical ways to deal with loneliness, ways that work once we try them.

Practical Ways to Deal with Loneliness

One thing is certain: when it comes to dealing with loneliness, we must be interested in life, interested in people, and not be shy and bashful. We need to make ourselves useful. Below is a list of some practical ways to do just that. It may be a big commitment, or it may be a smaller commitment. But remember, commitment is the key to connecting with people, even if we can't always be there in person. Use this handy reference whenever you start to feel lonely. Making plans is the first step to dealing with loneliness, and following through and taking action puts the gears in motion and shakes us out of our lonely and sometimes immobile state.

---

[8] See Matthew 22:37-39.

1.   **Volunteer** — I can tell you that whenever I have volunteered, I have always come away feeling that the reward is always greater than my efforts. Non-profit organizations depend on volunteers. In my hometown, it is a small group of hard-working volunteers that bring about all the social events for the town. Churches are run by volunteers. Even major sporting events, concerts, and other big happenings are run largely by volunteers. Volunteers are always needed. Just look in your local paper, or call your local town or city office, and they will supply you with a list of organizations looking for volunteers.

2.   **Pray** — Start your day in prayer. Make a list of 5 to 10 people and fervently pray for them each day for a week, then make a new list the next week. If possible, follow up with a caring phone call to see how they're doing. Read Job 42:10 to see what happened to Job when he prayed for his friends.   You'll be amazed at how quickly your situation can and will change when you start praying for people.

3.   **Read** — Read your Bible and a devotional every day. Unlike other books, the Bible is the "living Word," and can change a life. The Lord will be there to share in your searching, and He'll teach you many wonderful things specifically for your particular situation. Also, read wholesome books and books you enjoy. It's the next best thing to enrolling in a course. If possible, lighten up your reading and read a cartoon or something funny. Develop a good sense of humor. Laughter has a healing power and can heal our bodies and our souls. Or, if you don't like reading, make some popcorn and invite a friend over to watch a funny (clean) movie together.

4.   **Keep a journal** — Writing out our thoughts and feelings can be very therapeutic. Sometimes when there is no one to bare our souls to (like late at night when we can't sleep), it's good to write everything out, read it over, then throw it away (or keep it if you like). When we write things down, we get a much clearer perspective on things, and we can sometimes see how foolish we are or how menial our problems

are once they're written down. Or we can keep a journal of all the good things that happen to us and then go back and re-read how good God is and how wonderful our life really is and has been.

5. **Pursue hobbies** — There are dozens of hobbies available to us that can be fun, enjoyable, and definitely take our minds off ourselves. Some women I know sew, knit, and crochet beautiful quilts for needy families that have newborns or families that need bedding. Some people are into scrap-booking; they take all their old photos and make an interesting photo album of memories for each of their children that will be cherished forever. My husband enjoys fine woodworking and creating art carvings out of wood. I have a long list of hobbies I enjoy, including jewelry making, sewing, photography, and fine art painting. I can't tell you the many hours I've happily spent creating something that I later give away or sell in a craft show.

6. **Join a Bible class or take a course** — Bible studies will enrich our spiritual and social life. Many friendships are made at Bible Studies. It is easy to let our minds stagnate and rehearse the same thoughts over and over again. Taking a course in something will freshen our thoughts and expand our small world. Learning keeps our brain cells producing more brain cells — this may even stave off not only loneliness, but depression and early Alzheimer's disease.

7. **Mentor younger people** — Mentoring the younger seems to be an almost lost tradition today. And in some cases, we expect the younger to cater to us and care for us as we age. But this is not even mentioned in the Bible. Rather, the older are supposed to be an example and teach the younger (see Titus 2:2-5). Young people today need support and to hear wise counsel more than ever before. Many of them are lost and searching, not knowing right from wrong or which way to turn. There is tremendous opportunity to mentor young people and be available to them as someone who will listen, care, and be there for them when they need a listening ear or loving hug. It is easy to help our own children and grandchildren, but what

about those kids that have no one to turn to? They need us just as much as our own family needs us, maybe more. Be the one they can turn to.

8. <u>**Pet-wise**</u> — Studies have shown that pets actually can prolong a lonely person's life. They take an investment in time, money, and sometimes aggravation, but the rewards are too numerous to mention. If you don't want a pet of your own or can't have one where you live, consider volunteering to pet-sit when friends or acquaintances with pets go away on vacation. I know that when my husband and I have needed a pet-sitter for our cats, we had a friend who was always willing to check in on them. Her willingness to do this meant everything to us, and it's not always easy to rely on people with their busy schedules to come once a day to care for a pet.

9. <u>**Physical exercise, diet, and rest**</u> — Join a health club, or if you can't afford this, ask a friend to join you and go for a walk. If you like sports, take up golfing, swimming, or racquet sports. If you dislike physical exercise and sports, go and watch the local kids play. In every rink or ball field, there is always a spirited energy and mutual feeling of anticipation to see which team will win. Sports-players always enjoy a good audience, and they'll appreciate your support and encouragement.

<u>**Diet**</u> — If you like cooking, invite a friend over to enjoy a delicious bowl of soup with you or take a casserole over to someone who is also alone or too busy or sick to prepare a meal. Sharing a meal or coffee and a muffin is one of the most heart-warming times of fellowship we can ever know. This is when we mutually relax, enjoy, and really communicate with one another.

<u>**Rest**</u> — Get a good night's sleep. Go to bed early even if you don't sleep right away. Read or watch a good movie until you fall asleep. You'll feel so much better in the morning.

10. <u>**Phone Calls & Emails**</u> — If you are unwell or unable to get out, pick up the phone and call someone, or send them an email. You'd be surprised how much people in a similar situation as your own appreciate your thoughtfulness. Better yet, call your local florist and send someone a bouquet of flowers with a thoughtful card. These are the kinds of things people never forget, and by lifting someone else's spirits, you'll be lifting up your own.

You can probably add to this list, but the most important thing is to pick something that interests you and start getting active. You don't have to be going out somewhere to be active. It can all start with just picking up the phone and calling someone. We never need to feel that we're trapped. Freedom from the pain of loneliness is available to us in so many creative ways, we can have fun just going down the list and picking and choosing which one we'll do first. Above all, don't let loneliness overcome you — look at loneliness, especially the times you feel the pain, stress, and sadness of it, not as something you have to endure, but as an opportunity to make a new friend. There are times when it's necessary to take a firm stand and determine to make some good changes in your life.

In the final chapter, we'll talk about how we can come to the place of peace and rest and find fulfilment; ultimately, how to move from unhealthy isolation and solitude to enjoy the journey of our life.

Chapter 5
Enjoying the Journey

In this chapter we're going to talk about coming face to face, not with loneliness, but with ourselves. Self is sometimes our greatest roadblock on the road to happiness and fulfilment in our lives, whether we go it alone or not. Sometimes we can be our own worst enemy. There are many roadblocks we set up, so we can't really enjoy the journey through life that we are meant to enjoy to the fullest. For instance, we don't think highly enough of ourselves or we think too highly of ourselves, which affects all our relationships. Also, often what accompanies loneliness is depression. If we are feeling down, it is unlikely we'll want to go out or burden someone else with our problems, and so our loneliness intensifies. And some people do not want to hear about our troubles over and over again, especially if we seem to be continuously in a state of anxiety and need. People have enough of their own troubles, and they often can't handle any more. This is where professional assistance can greatly assist us, whether it's a pastor of a church or a trained counselor or psychologist. One thing is certain — once we've dealt with self and quieted all its demands, we can begin to enjoy relationships and enjoy the unique journey of our life — with or without a plethora of friends.

What to do with Self?

Is it wrong to feel lonely and want to find ways to overcome loneliness? Certainly not. There's nothing wrong with being lonely. But "self" sometimes handles things in a wrong way. In my case, I've been impatient, angry, and self-willed, determined to find my way out of loneliness in my own way and in my own time. This is "self" being demanding and in control, rather than submitting my weakness and problem to the Lord and letting Him be in control.

I believe the Lord allowed me to experience deep loneliness because I needed to come face to face with some major issues that were affecting my life and would continue to affect me until they were dealt with. Wanting to be in control was probably the greatest detriment I ever struggled with, and this is what the Lord wanted to deal with (and continues to) in my life. Of course, the Lord can strip away anything from us in order to get our full and undivided attention. For me, I had to be humbled and quieted, and so I found myself alone more often than not. In these quiet times, I learned more about myself and the Lord than at any other time, even while studying as a Bible school student. I learned the art of not only praying but listening as well. Now, I probably listen even more than I pray, because I know the Lord is near and He will answer me with a perfect answer to whatever situation I am facing.

I had a good friend in the city who I used to confide in when I was going through these difficult, lonely times. He would always encourage me, and one time he pointed out that feeling lonely or depressed, rather than being a negative thing, was actually a very positive thing. Then he shared about the apostle Paul's besetting problem:

> *And lest I should be exalted above measure through the abundance of the revelations, there was given to me a thorn in the flesh, the messenger of Satan to buffet me, lest I should be exalted above measure. For this thing I besought the Lord thrice, that it might depart from me. And he said unto me, <u>My grace is sufficient for thee: for my strength is made perfect in weakness</u>. Most gladly therefore will I rather glory in my infirmities, that the power of Christ may rest upon me. Therefore I take pleasure in infirmities, in reproaches, in necessities, in persecutions, in distresses for Christ's sake: for when I am weak, then am I strong. 2 Corinthians 12:7-10*

There is something in the Bible applicable to every situation in our lives, and this passage of Scripture literally changed my life and how I viewed my besetting problems from that point on. Sometimes our besetting "thorn in the flesh" will not go away no matter how hard we pray for it to disappear. Why? Because God is going to use it for His glory, and in the case of loneliness, which doesn't easily go away, it can actually strengthen us because it is a weakness. This is the time we reach out to God and then grow leaps and bounds in our faith. Also, for me, it has resulted in a much closer walk with the Lord. I've had to ask myself — What is my goal in not wanting to be alone? I've had to find answers that are honest, and the Lord has revealed a hidden agenda that had everything to do with self and selfish ambition. During these quiet times of revelation and discovery, it has felt like a wilderness experience with no crutches to lean on, except the enduring, loving support of the Lord.

In my 20s, after I lost my room-mate because she got married, I was faced with living alone. During these years, I discovered some of the magnitude of the multi-tasking of the Lord and the many different roles He fulfills — for me He's been a faithful Comforter, Counselor, Best Friend, Brother, Father, Nurse, Teacher, Advisor, and more. Whatever the situation, He can fulfil it. I learned to depend on Him, lean heavily on Him, and let Him bear my burdens. One of the most difficult times of day for me was bedtime. But I developed a routine of writing in my journal, making a list of the next day's activities, then reading the Word and praying. My mind would be clear, and I'd be able to go to bed knowing also that I was prepared for the next day. I'd go to bed with such peace in my heart. Many nights I felt that the Lord was literally cradling me to sleep. He truly is a Friend that sticks closer than a brother (see Proverbs 18:24b). I have learned that loneliness can strengthen you like nothing else can, and when it seems like a great weakness, the Lord can use it for His glory.

Emotional Housecleaning

At one point, after I had broken up with Eric, I needed to seek professional help to get my life back on track. I really wanted to be healthy emotionally so that I could move forward in my life. I wanted stability so I could commit to a good job and one day be prepared to be married. I was advised to attend a 12-step program designed for people with emotional weaknesses. It was truly one of the best groups I ever attended. Throughout each step, it encouraged me to meet myself head on — face-to-face. It was unnerving at first, but with a group of courageous, loving people surrounding me who would never judge or repeat anything I shared, it was one of the most healing experiences of my entire life. I only wish more people would reach out to such a group and find the kind of support I had.

The program shows you how to take a good, honest look at yourself. We soon discover that the reason we struggle with besetting emotional problems is because we usually don't want to accept responsibility for our feelings or actions, so we continue making the same mistake over and over again, and we become ensnared by it. It is much easier to blame someone or something else than admit we made some unhealthy choices along the way. Without feeling threatened, guilty, or remorseful, I was shown how to really uncover the root causes of my anxiety and depression. When it was uncovered, I didn't at all like some of the things I saw looking back at me. I had to list all the times I ever felt hurt or wronged by someone, which was easy enough to do; but the really difficult part was to also list how I had reacted to those who had hurt or wronged me.

In a church we once attended, we prayed the Lord's Prayer every Sunday. It's easy to say, "Forgive us our trespasses as we forgive those who trespass against us," in a general prayer, but try writing down the details of each and every person who has trespassed against you for as far back as you can remember, and then list your own reaction (or retribution) to each of those situations — that takes a lot of honesty and soul-searching. I made my long list, and then I had to share it with someone I had never met before who acts as a non-partial counselor. The next step was to make amends to the people that had hurt me or that I had hurt, even if it was just my reaction to them hurting me. I never realized how resentful I had felt towards people who had hurt me in the past, and I never realized how resentment stays with us until we actually uncover our true feelings by writing them down. I made some amends by writing letters, others by phone call, and those I couldn't reach by praying from my heart. Then I destroyed the list.

I really had no idea how freeing this was. I have had the joyous experience of being born-again in my spiritual life, but when I did this, I felt similar, in that I was able to put the past behind me and move forward without all the emotional junk weighing me down as it had been for all those years. My emotional house had been completely swept clean, and I felt like a new person, with no hurts of the past to haunt me, no more angry outbursts, and nothing to be depressed about. And I also discovered my strengths and weaknesses, which I discussed with this same counselor who had heard my hurts. This was also freeing, since from now on, Satan could no longer accuse me of something I had already confessed and been forgiven for. I actually started to like myself, who I was and who the Lord had created. They say that if you don't like yourself, other people won't like you either. Well now, it didn't matter to me what other people thought — I liked myself, and I knew I was forgiven; God loves me — and that's all that matters.

Get Rid of Compromise

It is far better to be alone than to sell our souls to the wrong crowd or the wrong person in order to not "feel" lonely. Self has an agenda to "get something," and this is its greatest downfall, because in order to get something, there is always a cost. Nowhere is this clearer than in an old 1941 movie called *The Devil and Daniel Webster*. A hard-luck farmer, Jabez Stone, is enticed to sell his soul to the devil for prosperity. More than losing his soul, he loses his wife, family, and friends and on the eve of the pay-back for his soul, when he will die and go to hell, he realizes too late what a terrible cost he has to pay.

Yes, there is a cost for being lonely, but when our attentions are directed to a good cause, there is also great reward, especially if we seek the Lord's guidance and direction during these times. But if we use this time for self and selfish gain, we will find ourselves alone again and again, because the wrong kind of relationships, empty activity void of good works, and striving for things that can never satisfy will continue to disappoint us.

In my own life, one of the greatest ways I have dealt with loneliness is to have a purpose and a goal in mind each and every day. I work at home most of the time, so I have a pretty good idea of what I'll be doing each day. If you work at home and for your own business, it can be pretty easy to stray and do something else, but you soon discover that watching TV or calling your friends does not get the work done. Then you have to work twice as hard the next day to catch up. It takes discipline to live alone and work alone. Compromising valuable time will eat away at every good purpose if we let it.

I remember times when I lived alone in the city that although I had a purpose (writing), I didn't have the discipline to follow through, and so I never completed my books. I compromised my time by shopping, pursuing sports, hobbies, special interest courses, and socializing. There are worse compromises that we can make when we are lonely and especially when we lack purpose. I have talked to many an unhappy spouse who married out of haste and realized that when two people disagree, especially on core spiritual beliefs, the marriage cannot work. One time when I was between jobs, I was working at temporary clerical jobs, and I met a Christian girl who was dating a non-Christian man. When I asked her about it, she said, "Oh, I gave up on waiting for a Christian man. If you wait for that, you'll never get married." Her words were tempting to me since I kind of wondered if she was right since it seemed that all the eligible men around my age (late 20s) were already married and some already divorced. My situation seemed bleak indeed, especially when I realized that I would have to wait and trust God to provide a husband in His time rather than me going out to try and find him. But God knew that a little loneliness would be far better than a lifetime of regret and sorrow. I'm so glad I waited even though it seemed a long wait; it was worth it all.

Compromise, whether it's a matter of our faith or whether we get involved with the wrong kind of person, can easily happen when we feel alone, vulnerable, afraid, and insecure. This is why a personal relationship with the Lord Jesus Christ, first and foremost, is essential, not only to set us on the right course for the rest of our lives, but to secure our place in heaven when it is our time to die. Out of this spiritual rebirth, many wonderful life-time friendships are made as we seek fellowship and then make commitments to be involved in people's lives in a way that is pleasing to God.

There is an acronym that is used for people who are likely to compromise when any of the following are present. It is HALT. H — Hungry; A — Angry; L — Lonely; T — Tired. If I feel any of those things, beware; I am more likely to compromise. Alcoholics are more likely to start drinking, drug addicts to take drugs, and so on. I wonder how many people are out there who feel this way every day? These are the very same people the Lord would have us show compassion to — to feed the hungry, to listen to a troubled or angry soul, to be a friend to someone in need, and to provide a place of rest to someone who is tired.[9] If my purpose is to be available to those the

---

[9] See Matthew 25:35-40.

Lord would show compassion to, then I must allow Him to love them through me and offer them the resources He has loaned me. Then I won't feel the pain of loneliness any more, and the journey of my life will be filled with bouquets of God's enduring promises, with God Himself as my constant guide and willing companion.

I trust that you have discovered and will continue to discover that loneliness can be a most welcome friend, an eyeglass into our souls, a shining lantern in the night enlightening our way, and a friendly beacon throughout the storms of our weary days. May you continue on this pathway of discovery and enjoy the journey, whatever path you find yourself on today.

The Way of Salvation

In all of life, no one loves you more than God does. He loved you so much He sent His own Son to die on a cross, then He raised Him up again, and He lives forevermore. When Jesus died, a phenomenal thing happened — He willingly took all our sins and sicknesses upon Himself so that we wouldn't have to bear them ourselves. He forgave us the huge debt of sin we owed to God, so that we could be pardoned and set free to live a life unto Him. Salvation is free and open to all who call upon the name of the only One who can truly save us. If you haven't already taken this important step, you are invited to accept Jesus into your heart and life today. Begin by reading the following Scriptures to begin your new life, and don't delay!

Today is the day of salvation ...

> *(For he saith, I have heard thee in a time accepted, and in the day of salvation have I succoured thee: behold, now is the accepted time; behold, now is the day of salvation.) 2 Corinthians 6:2*

We are all in need of salvation ...

> *For all have sinned, and come short of the glory of God; Romans 3:23*

Good works cannot save you ...

> *They are all gone out of the way, they are together become unprofitable; there is none that doeth good, no, not one. Romans 3:12*

> *Not by works of righteousness which we have done, but according to his mercy he saved us, by the washing of regeneration, and renewing of the Holy Ghost; Titus 3:5*

The Lord will never turn away anyone who truly wants to know Him ...

For whosoever shall call upon the name of the Lord shall be saved. Romans 10:13

Jesus is the only One who can save us ...

Neither is there salvation in any other: for there is none other name under heaven given among men, whereby we must be saved. Acts 4:12

That at the name of Jesus every knee should bow, of things in heaven, and things in earth, and things under the earth; Philippians 2:10

Salvation gives us eternal life with Jesus ...

For God so loved the world, that he gave his only begotten Son, that whosoever believeth in him should not perish, but have everlasting life. John 3:16

For God sent not his Son into the world to condemn the world; but that the world through him might be saved. John 3:17

But every person is condemned without Jesus ...

He that believeth on him is not condemned: but he that believeth not is condemned already, because he hath not believed in the name of the only begotten Son of God. John 3:18

We have an assurance of salvation ...

And I give unto them eternal life; and they shall never perish, neither shall any man pluck them out of my hand. John 10:28

My Father, which gave them me, is greater than all; and no man is able to pluck them out of my Father's hand. John 10:29

Dear Friend,

If you would like to receive Jesus into your heart and life today and also have the assurance that you will spend eternity in heaven with Him, please begin by saying this prayer:

Dear Heavenly Father,

I come to you in the name of Jesus. Your Word says, "Whosoever shall call upon the name of the Lord shall be saved" (Acts 2:21). I call on you now, and ask Jesus to come into my heart, forgive me for all my sins, and cleanse me. I ask you to be Lord over my life, according to Romans 10:9-10 — "That if thou shalt confess with thy mouth the Lord Jesus, and shalt believe in thine heart that God hath raised him from the dead, thou shalt be saved. For with the heart man believeth unto righteousness; and with the mouth confession is made unto salvation." I do this now — I confess that Jesus is Lord, and I believe in my heart that God raised Him from the dead.

In Jesus Name,
Amen

You are now reborn! You are a Christian and a child of God! Be assured, you have taken the most important step of your life, and God has reserved your place in heaven. He will always be with you, and lead you into all truth:

But the Comforter, which is the Holy Ghost, whom the Father will send in my name, he shall teach you all things, and bring all things to your remembrance, whatsoever I have said unto you. John 14:26

...for he hath said, I will never leave thee, nor forsake thee. Hebrews 13:5b

You will need to read the Bible on a daily basis to get to know Him, and all the many promises He has for you. As well, don't delay in contacting a Bible-believing church, where you will find fellowship with others who have also taken this important life-changing step. May God bless you as you continue on your new path of life, and freedom in Christ!

About the Author

Linda McBurney-Gunhouse enjoys her life in Manitoba, Canada. She writes to help others and inspire them to overcome difficulties and achieve success in life. She also enjoys story-telling in the form of writing fiction. Linda has spent a life-time writing and honing her skills. She studied Journalism, English, and History and received both a BA and B.Ed. in English. She has a diploma in magazine writing. She has worked as a contributing editor for a community college newspaper, and also as an editor for a community newspaper in Winnipeg. Her articles have appeared in national, city, and community newspapers and one magazine. She has written and sold one radio play. She is an accomplished eBook author of several inspirational books, including five full-length fiction. Her readership is international, and some of her eBooks frequently reach the Top 100 in specific categories. Linda also writes thought-provoking blogs.

Linda loves to share her faith and how she has overcome the many challenges in life in a way that readers can relate to. She sometimes teaches Creative Writing, and she does special speaking. Occasionally, she does free-lance writing for the local newspapers. She has also facilitated her own online and in-person writers' group. She continues to expand her thought-provoking blogs and book-writing. When she is not writing, she loves to be involved in creating art.

Other Titles

By Linda McBurney-Gunhouse

Inspirational Books

Cures for Stress
Essential Steps to Increase Your Faith
Footpath to Freedom
Freedom Through Spiritual Discernment
Healing & Hope for Child Loss
Healing For The Wounded Soul
Loneliness: The Pathway to Discovery
Making Sense of the Rapture
Money: Master or Servant?
No Fear of Hell
Power Thoughts for Positive Thinking
Spiritual Leadership in a Fallen World
The Act of Decision-Making
The Bible: Conformed or Transformed?
The Journey of Oneness
The Journey to Contentment
The Power of Submission
Victory Over Backsliding
When Love Is All There Is

Biography

The Bonk Saga: A History of Memories
Called to Overcome

Devotionals

Pathways to Devotion I
Pathways to Devotion II
Pathways to Devotion III
Pathways to Devotion IV
Pathways to Devotion V
Pathways to Devotion VI
Pathways to Devotion VII
Pathways to Devotion VIII
Pathways to Devotion IX
Pathways to Devotion X
Pathways to Devotion XI
Pathways to Devotion XII

Fiction

The Redemption of Steep Rock Cove
Return to Steep Rock Cove
Christmas Comes to Steep Rock Cove
Waves of Change at Steep Rock Cove
Driving with the Top Down
Track Three
Joanna's Secret Treasure

Poetry Books

Heart Songs
Songs in the Desert
Water Crossings
Wings I: Morning Arising
Wings II: Daylight Reflections
Wings III: Contemplation
Wings: Inspirational Poetry Series

Creative How-to Books

Artistic Ideas & Inspirations
How to Create Stories From Your Own Life
Living a Creative Life

Writing Manuals

Creative Writing
Write Your Life Story
Fiction Writing

Please visit our website at www.creativefocus.ca to discover the many books from this list that are available as eBooks.

Note: If you have enjoyed reading this book, or any other eBook of mine, please rate it online, or recommend it on your Facebook page. It will help spread the word, and let others know it is available. My goal is to help, encourage and inspire others through my writing. Thank you and may God richly bless you!

www.ingramcontent.com/pod-product-compliance
Lightning Source LLC
Chambersburg PA
CBHW070459050426
42449CB00012B/3040